I. Introduction

The Sherman Antitrust Act is now more than a century old, yet debate still continues about its original goals. Previous authors, focusing on the substance of the 1890 debate, have reached various conclusions about these goals. Each of these conclusions provides different implications for antitrust policy. Currently, the debate focuses on whether the purpose of the Sherman Act is to maximize economic efficiency or the welfare of consumers. The aim of this paper is to reach beyond the rhetoric and discuss the institutional context of the Sherman Act to discern between these two hypotheses. This analysis will imply that the primary goal of the Sherman Act was to promote economic efficiency.

The weight of the evidence, however, suggests that, at least in the later years of the Reagan and early years of the Bush Administrations, the Federal government has applied a welfare of consumers standard.[1] Scholarly support for this position is provided by Lande (1982), who used the context of the Congressional debates to assert that preventing transfers of wealth from consumers to producers was the primary goal of the Sherman Act. (See also Fisher and Lande, 1983, and Fisher, Johnson, and Lande, 1989). In contrast, Bork (1966)

---

[1] For example, then-FTC Chairman Oliver (1988) endorsed a "price test" by identifying the role of the FTC as preventing price increases or output reductions, which is equivalent to a welfare of consumers standard. Current FTC Chairman Janet Steiger ("Agenda For the Federal Trade Commission," Remarks of Janet Steiger before the 23rd New England Antitrust Conference, Cambridge MA, November 3, 1989, reprinted in 57 <u>Antitrust and Trade Regulation Report</u> 674, November 9, 1989) has stated that maximizing the welfare of consumers is the appropriate goal of antitrust policy. The 1992 Department of Justice and Federal Trade Commission Horizontal Merger Guidelines, 4 Trade Regulation Reporter (CCH) 13104, at Section 0.1, describes the adverse results of the exercise of market power to be "a transfer of wealth from buyers to sellers <u>or</u> a misallocation of resources" (emphasis added, the "or" representing a change from the "and" in the 1984 Guidelines). Constantine (1990 at 168-9) asserts that the welfare of consumers standard is used by the state attorneys general. Under this standard if as a result of a merger or competitive practice, price to consumers rises, then *ceteris paribus*, consumers (and not necessarily society) are harmed and government intervention is appropriate. For a discussion of Lande's influence on this debate, see Kovacic (1990 at 1462-3).

inferred from the same evidence that economic efficiency was the goal of the Sherman Act. Section II will discuss the difference between an efficiency and a welfare-of-consumers standard.

While examining congressional rhetoric is important to determining the intent of the authors of the Act, it is not the only available instrument. Indeed, the congressional oratory would likely have been largely the same whether the intent of the Sherman Act was economic efficiency or the welfare-of-consumers. Instead of concentrating on the congressional debates, this paper will examine the structural and historical context of the Sherman Act. Section III will argue that the Act is best viewed as a modest statutory extension of the common law. The goals of the common law will be discussed from the viewpoint of the "Law and Economics" school of analysis, and the substance of the congressional debates on the Sherman Act will also be analyzed from this perspective. This perspective will be used to generate a straightforward refutation of Lande's analysis.

Section IV will review the political support for the Act, the manner in which Congress chose to have the act administered, and later decisions Congress made in creating the Federal Trade Commission. The modern theory of interest groups and administrative agencies yields additional insight into the goals of the Act. The common law origins of antitrust, the support for, and implementation of the Act all support the conclusion that the primary goal of the Sherman Act was economic efficiency.

II. The Difference Between Economic Efficiency and the Welfare-of-Consumers

A. The Williamsonian Trade-off

"Economic efficiency" may in one sense be considered an economic term of art. The textbook conditions needed to generate efficiency are often quite complicated. On the other hand, economic efficiency is a simple idea. An action is "economically efficient" if it increases an economy's wealth, regardless of distributional considerations. Of course, no government intervention can be expected to generate mathematical optimality. The question addressed here is whether one particular law, the Sherman Act, was designed to reach toward economic efficiency, seeking to maximize the total wealth of society, or simply to maximize the welfare-of-consumers.

This trade-off between market power and economic efficiency was first formally described by Williamson (1968 at 21). Figure 1 is a slightly modified version of Williamson's Figure 1. Assume that there are only two (identical) firms in an industry and that they vigorously compete so that each is selling at price equal to (marginal and) average costs. Each firm has average costs as denoted by the line AC_1. Given the demand curve D, industry price equals P_1 and output equals Q_1. Now suppose that the two firms merge. The merger generates efficiencies that lower the combined firm's average costs to AC_2. Due to the lack of competition, however, the combined firm raises price to P_2 and lowers quantity to Q_2). As a result, consumers lose the rectangle A, which is wealth transferred to producers. They also lose the triangle B, which is the deadweight loss to society resulting from the allocative inefficiency of monopoly. The monopoly firm gains directly from the pockets of consumers the rectangle A. It also gains the rectangle C, which represents the costs savings due to the merger-related efficiencies. If C (the efficiency gain) is of greater size than B (the

3

Figure 1

The Williamson Tradeoff

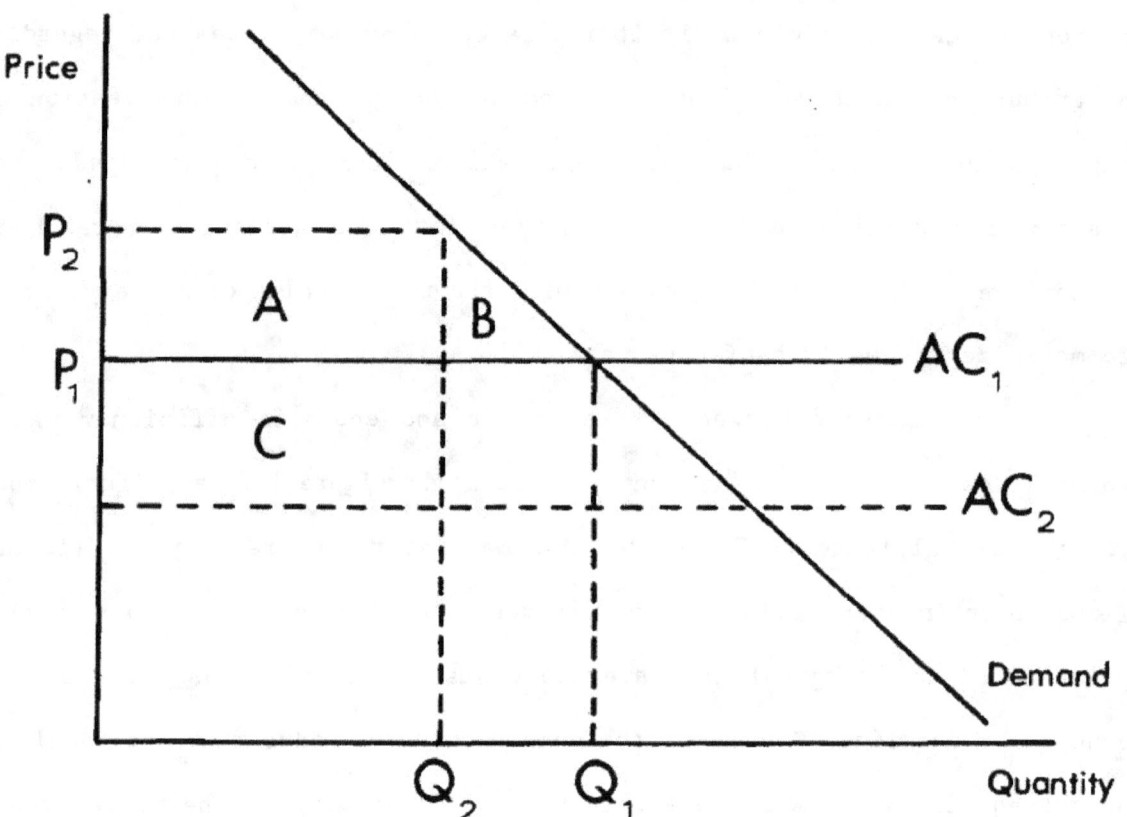

deadweight loss due to market power) then the merger would increase economic efficiency while decreasing the welfare-of-consumers.[2]

Following Bork, Williamson assumes (1968 at 21-22) that efficiency is the goal of the Sherman Act. Given this assumption, he generates broad measures of classes of mergers that generate market power but should be not opposed by the antitrust authorities because they would increase economic efficiency. In general, he determines that relatively small percentage levels of cost savings are necessary to offset the distortion arising from the exercise of market power. For example, Williamson (1968 at 32) shows that the welfare loss associated with a 20 percent price increase would be offset by efficiencies of 4 percent for a price elasticity of two and 2 percent for an elasticity of one.[3]

B. Lande Versus Bork on the Congressional Debates

Bork's conclusion that efficiency is the goal of antitrust has come under attack during the last several years. Using the debate over the Sherman Act as his guide, Lande presents three arguments why the welfare-of-consumers, rather than economic efficiency, was the congressional goal of the antitrust laws.

First, Congress spent the bulk of the debate discussing consumer welfare (or, as Lande puts it, the "welfare-of-consumers"). No individual Congressmen expressed explicit interest in having the Act promote the goal of economic

---

[2] Because the monopoly firm raises price, it increases its own profits. Posner (1975) contends that these profits will be dissipated in rent seeking activities as colluding firms seek to capture profits. (Posner does not seem to address anticompetitive actions by dominant firms, which is the example used by Williamson.) Williamson (1977 at 713) argues that "rent seeking" in the form of competition would generate entry and thus only part of these profits should be counted as social costs of monopoly.

[3] For extended discussions of Williamson's analysis, see Fisher and Lande (1983 at 1624-61) and Fisher, Johnson, and Lande (1988 at 788-90).

efficiency (Lande, 1982 at 94-95). Second, Congress was generally motivated to pass redistributive, rather than pro-efficiency laws (Lande 1982 at 77 and 88). Finally, Lande (1982 at 88) argues that Congress was unfamiliar with the concept of economic efficiency. Lande asserts that, since the term "economic efficiency" was known to very few in 1890, Congress could not have been trying to achieve it.

Because Congress did not know about economic efficiency, Lande concludes that it could not have intended for the Sherman Act to combat the welfare reductions generated by monopoly. He thus infers that the goal of the antitrust laws is to maximize the welfare-of-consumers. The gains from eliminating deadweight loss triangles are merely incidental, since Congress was not aware of their existence. Lande (1982 at 126) uses similar analysis to reach the same conclusions with respect to the FTC and the Clayton Acts.

Bork also points out that Congress spent most of the debate discussing consumer welfare. In fact, Bork and Lande largely agree on the content of the Congressional debate. The major difference between the two is that Bork (1966 at 7) equates consumer welfare with economic efficiency. He does this by implicitly arguing that producers are also consumers. This led Lande to redefine consumer welfare as "the welfare-of-consumers," a term equivalent in economic jargon to "consumers' surplus." This article does not review in detail the nature of the debates over the Sherman Act. Instead, it will assume that Bork and Lande were correct in their conclusions that consumer welfare (however defined) was the primary topic of discussion in the debates.

The difference between rectangles and triangles has significant implications for antitrust policy. For instance, as Fisher, Johnson, and Lande (1989) illustrate, under a welfare-of-consumers standard, the market concentration levels that would trigger a merger challenge are significantly lower than under an efficiency standard. A welfare-of-consumers standard also generates a stronger rationale for enforcement of provisions against "tying" and price discrimination, practices with ambiguous welfare effects that benefit producers and thus may harm consumers. The narrow welfare-of-consumers standard has thus become an argument for a more stringent and activist antitrust policy.

C. Consumer Welfare and the Welfare-of-Consumers: Is There Really Any Difference?

Lande's term "the welfare-of-consumers" draws a distinction between consumer and producer welfare. Following on Bork, Calvani (1984) argues that this is a false dichotomy. He reasons that the owners of producer's surplus (stockholders) are consumers as well, and therefore any monopoly profits generated by anticompetitive activities are eventually redistributed to consumers.

Examining the Congressional debates to determine whether Congress was interested in the welfare-of-consumers narrowly defined or consumer welfare as economic efficiency would appear to be a difficult exercise. Any conclusion that could be reached would be based on nuances of rhetoric. It seems reasonable, however, to assume that Congress knew that corporations, the primary beneficiaries of monopoly, were owned by individual consumers in the form of stockholders. It could be that Congress sought to redistribute income away from the wealthier stockholder class, but Lande (1982 at 70) rejects this hypothesis.

Similarly, Easterbrook (1986 at 1703) argues that in the long run an efficiency standard is the proper measure of the welfare-of-consumers. In the long run all firms compete for the opportunity to gain monopoly profits and therefore all monopoly profits are eventually competed away in the form of new entry. This implies that long-run producer surplus is zero and all monopoly profits are eventually redistributed back to consumers in the form of increased entry and innovation by would-be monopolists. (For a survey of the relevant economic literature see Shoven and Whalley, 1984.)

The (apparent) logical answer to this line of analysis, though Lande does not make it, is that Congress was not that interested in the long run. Modern public choice scholars (for example, Tollison and McCormick, 1981 at 68) argue that political actors have higher implicit discount rates for future events than economic actors. Thus, Congress may not have been willing to wait for the long run for these economic profits to be redistributed.[4]

To summarize, Lande's "welfare-of-consumers" argument rests on two necessary, but not sufficient, conditions. First, it assumes that Congress did not include the owners of capital in its definition of consumers. Second, it assumes that Congress was myopic (that is, it employed a higher discount rate than society) in its construction of economic policy. While both assumptions appear defensible, though by no means impregnable, they have not been properly addressed by Lande. Put another way, employing Lande's narrow "welfare-of-consumers" standard implies maximizing the short-run welfare of those who buy a particular product and ignoring the welfare of all other parties.

III. The Antitrust Laws and the Common Law

The Sherman Act did not mark a revolutionary change in competition law. Rather, scholars are clear that the Sherman Act was a logical extension of the centuries-old common law in restraint of trade. The restraint of trade caselaw

---

[4] This argument will be refuted in Section III-B below and thus may be considered a "straw man." There is, however, no other defense on this issue apparent to this author.

is consistent with how the "Law and Economics" paradigm predicts the common law will evolve towards economic efficiency. Using this background, Lande's conclusion as to the "welfare-of-consumers" is shown to have a number of logical difficulties. Instead, the analysis of the legal origins of the Sherman Act will be shown to support the hypothesize that the goal of the Sherman Act is to promote economic efficiency.

A. The Sherman Act as an Extension of the Common Law

1. The Common Law Background of Antitrust

Antitrust law did not begin in 1890 with the Sherman Act. As numerous writers discuss, the common law opposition to restraint of trade dates back several centuries.[5] For instance, the rule of reason outlined by Chief Justice White in *U.S. v. Standard Oil* 221 U.S. 1 (1911), is an amalgamation of several common law cases, the most important being the 1711 British case *Mitchel v. Reynolds* 1, P. William 181. White's decision explained how both *per se* and rule-of-reason cases evolved under the common law and how those common law precedents fit naturally into antitrust enforcement under the Sherman Act. White wrote (at 58) that both the common law and the Sherman Act prohibited, "all contracts or acts which were unreasonably restrictive of competitive conditions, either from the nature or character of the contracts or acts [this refers to *per se* offenses] or where the surrounding circumstances were ... of such character as to give rise to the inference or presumption that they had been entered into with the intent to do wrong to the general public..." This characterization is not significantly

---

[5] A short list of such scholars would include Baxter (1982), Easterbrook (1986), Easton (1890), Letwin (1954), Oppenheim, Weston, and McCarthy (1981), Thorelli (1955), and Toulmine (1949), as well as Judge (later Chief Justice) Taft (whose *Addyston Pipe* decision is discussed below).

different from the one used by Chief Justice Parker in *Mitchel v. Reynolds* (at 190), "[i]n all restraints of trade where nothing more appears, the law presumes them bad; but if the circumstances are set forth, that presumption is excluded, and the Court is to judge of these circumstances, and determine accordingly ..."

Perhaps the most important antitrust tenet gained from the common law was the unenforceability of contracts that created restrictive arrangements. The seminal discussion of the common law's general opposition to collusive contracts is Judge William Howard Taft's opinion in *U.S. v. Addyston Pipe*, 85 F. 271 (6th Cir. 1898), *modified and aff'd*. 175 U.S. 211 (1899). In supporting the decision that led to the *per se* rule under the Sherman Act for "naked" restraints such as price-fixing, Taft refers to more than 100 common law restraint-of-trade cases in his decision.

The common law can be seen as a framework for giving consumers property rights to "competitively" priced goods to generate efficient economic outcomes. Unfortunately, the common law, by itself, does not appear to have been sufficient for the task of dealing with the anticompetitive problems generated by the Industrial Revolution.

2. How the Sherman Act Strengthened the Common Law

There were instances prior to the Sherman Act where the common law was used to fight anticompetitive actions. In general, however, it was not well suited to this task. In the age of industrialization, the common law in the United States faced three serious problems.

First, industrialization created barriers to entry and economies of scale, increasing the opportunity for the exercise of market power. (See, for example, Oppenheim, Weston, and McCarthy, 1981.) Coupled with the advent of the railroad, industrialization made interstate commerce more frequent and therefore more important. No federal restraint of trade common law existed in the U.S. prior to the enactment of the Sherman Act. Common law at the state level did not protect interstate commerce from anticompetitive practices that the Industrial Revolution had made more likely. While there were a number of state cases, in general the states had difficulty reaching broad areas of commerce.[6]

Second, the existing tort law was not comprehensive in its handling of antitrust matters. The general unenforceability of anticompetitive agreements among producers under the common contract law discouraged their use. But where such agreements could succeed without enforcement through the courts, consumers had no cause of action to challenge their use. The common law could have evolved towards giving consumers a cause of action, but legislators were unwilling to wait.

Third, private antitrust enforcement may suffer from a public goods problem. While a few sellers may gain handsomely from a successful cartel, the losses may be spread among perhaps millions of consumers. No one consumer, or even perhaps a coalition of thousands of consumers, may have sufficient incentives to bring legal action, because they would bear all of the costs and gain only part of the benefit, even after compensating for the treble damages available in private suits. Thus, legal challenge by individuals or groups of individuals to monopoly would be likely to be undersupplied.

The Sherman Act deals with these problems in perhaps the most concise

---

[6] For specific state cases, see *Attorney General v. American Sugar Refinery Co.*, 7 RY. & CORP. L.J. 83 (Cal. Super Ct. 1890) and *People v. North River Sugar Refining Co.* 121 N.Y. 582, 24 N.E. 798 (1889)). For a general discussion of both the scope and the limits of state antitrust enforcement see May (1987 at 507-520).

manner possible. First, it consists of a brief but vaguely worded statute[7] that creates a federal common law subject to interpretation by the judiciary to deal with problems of "restraint of trade," a common law concept. Bork (1966 at 35-6 and 46) makes it clear that at least Senator Sherman felt that the Act should be administered in the same fashion as the common law, thus enabling the judiciary to determine which practices should and should not be allowed. Second, it gives consumers a right to challenge restraint of trade contracts in court. Instead of being merely unenforceable, it makes such contracts subject to prosecution. In Taft's words (*Addyston Pipe* at 279)

> The effect of the [Sherman Act] is to render such [restraint of trade] contracts unlawful in a positive sense, and punishable as a misdemeanor, and to create a right of civil action for damages in favor of those injured thereby, and a civil remedy by injunction in favor of both private persons and the public against the execution of such contracts and the maintenance of such trade restraints.

Third, the Sherman Act paved the way for the establishment of a public prosecutor to address the public goods problem.[8] The Department of Justice, and later the Federal Trade Commission, could act as a public agent to stop or prevent

---

[7] Section 1 of the Act states, "Every contract, combination in the form of trust or otherwise, or conspiracy in restraint of trade or commerce among the several states, or with foreign nations, is declared to be illegal ," while Section 2 states "Every person who shall monopolize or attempt to monopolize, or combine or conspire with any other person or persons, to monopolize any part of the trade or commerce among the several states, or with foreign nations, shall be deemed guilty of a felony." 15 U.S.C. 1 and 2. As Lande (1982 at 81) points out, "[t]he antitrust laws are among the least precise statutes enacted by Congress."

[8] There is debate in the academic literature whether and to what extent a public prosecutor is needed to enforce this type of law. See, for example, Friedman (1984).

producers from capturing the property rights of consumers through anticompetitive actions. Thus, the Sherman Act can be viewed as a modest innovation to the common law on restraint of trade.

B. Deriving the Goal of the Sherman Act from the Goal of the Common Law

1. The Goal of the Common Law

The "Law and Economics" School of the past twenty years has argued that the goal of the judicially-written common law is to reach toward economic efficiency.[9] According to this theory, inefficient common law rules are gradually replaced by more efficient rules. While others[10] argue that there are goals besides efficiency, the efficiency theory would seem to go a long way towards describing the evolutions of common law. Further, there does not appear to be any other competing positive theory of common law. Thus, if one believes that the Sherman Act is a logical extension of the common law (which seems generally accepted) and that the goal of the common law is economic efficiency (which is somewhat more disputed), one has sufficient evidence to at least suspect that the goal of the Sherman Act was to promote economic efficiency.[11]

While it is an outgrowth of the common law, the Sherman Act is a product of legislative action. The "Law and Economics" school often distinguishes between the

---

[9] The thinkings of this school are perhaps best represented in Posner (1986) although the idea of law as promoting what is now termed economic efficiency is often traced back at least to Holmes (1963, first published in 1881). Commons (1925) traces this idea back to the early 19th century writings of Jeremy Bentham. See also the symposium "Changes in the Common Law: Legal and Economic Perspectives," 9 Journal of Legal Studies (1980) 189.

[10] See, for example, "Symposium on Efficiency as a Legal Concern," 8 Hofstra Law Review 485 (1980).

[11] Under this theory, in the long run, antitrust law will seek to achieve economic efficiency no matter what scholars write today on the subject. The long run, however, could conceivably last several decades or even centuries.

goals of common law (efficiency) and statutory law (wealth transfers or rent-seeking) (See Posner, (1986, chapters 13 and 19). Rubin (1982, 1983) argues that this distinction between common and statutory law is misleading. He contends that laws created both by courts and legislatures prior to the systematic rise of well organized interests groups (about 1930) are more likely to be devoted to efficiency enhancement, while laws after that period are more likely to be devoted to rent seeking.[12] According to this theory, legislators have a basic general interest in economic efficiency that can be overcome by the efforts of interest groups.

Rubin further contends that what the Law and Economics school calls the "common law" is really a combination of common law with efficiency enhancing statutes in torts and property law passed largely during the 18th and 19th centuries. Certainly the antitrust laws are consistent with this description. Thus, using Rubin's theory, efficiency as the goal of antitrust is consistent with the goal of efficiency in a number of other legal areas.

2. The Evolution of Common Law Restraint of Trade Cases

A full discussion of how the common law of restraint of trade reached towards economic efficiency is well beyond the scope of this work. A brief examination of the evolution of common law rules regarding covenants not to compete and naked restraints such as price fixing, however, shows how the pre-Sherman Act restraint of trade caselaw fits into the Law and Economics framework of judge-written law generating legal rules that reach towards economic efficiency.

---

[12] Of course, there are exceptions to Rubin's rule, such as the establishments of tariffs and the Interstate Commerce Act in the 19th century (redistributing economic rents), and the Airline Deregulation Act of 1978 and the Motor Carrier Act of 1980 (generating economic efficiency). Rubin's theory is similar to Olson's (1965, 1982) thesis that over time legislation becomes less efficiency-enhancing as more and more interest groups affect the political process.

Prior to the seventeenth century, English courts appear to have invoked a *per se* rule against covenants not to compete.[13] In *Rogers v. Parrey*, 2 Bulst. 136, 80 Eng. Reg. 1012 (1613), however, the Court of the King's Bench distinguished between general restraints (involving the entire Kingdom) and partial restraints (relating to a particular town), with the latter being permitted.

Mitchel v. Reynolds (1711) involved the lease of a bakery that prevented the lessor from operating a competing bakery in the same parish, Chief Justice Parker explained the reasons for the law's general hostility towards restraint of trade contracts:

> First. The mischief which may arise from them (1) to the party by the loss of his livelihood and the subsistence of his family; (2) to the public by depriving it of an useful member. Another reason is the great abuses these voluntary restraints are liable to; as, for instance, from corporations who are perpetually laboring for exclusive advantages in trade and to reduce it into as few hands as possible.

(This reasoning was echoed by the Massachusetts Supreme Court in *Alger v. Thacher*, 19 Pick. 54 (1837).)

The efficiency reasons for allowing such covenants was expressed by Baron Parke in *Mallan v. May*, 11 Mees. & W. 652 (1843), who wrote about what now would be termed a "free-rider" defense:

> Contracts for the partial restraint of trade are upheld ... because it is for the benefit of the public at large that they should be enforced. ... Such is the case of disposing of a shop in a particular place with a contract on the part of the vendor not to carry on a trade in the same place. It is, in effect, the sale of

---

[13] See, for example, *The Dyer's Case*, Y.B. Pasch. 2 Hen. 5, f.5, pl 26 (1415), and *The Blacksmith's Case*, 2 Leo. 210, 3 Leo. 217 (1587). *Alger v. Thacher*, 19 Pick. 51, 52 (Mass., 1837), refers to the *per se* rule as being "old and settled law" by 1415.

a good will, and offers an encouragement to trade by allowing a
party to dispose of all of the fruits of his industry.... In such a
case the public derives an advantage in the unrestrained choice
which such a stipulation gives to the employer of able assistants
and the security it affords that the master will not withhold from
the servant instruction in the secrets of his trade, and the
communication of his own skill and experience, from the fear of his
afterwards having a rival in the same business.

Mitchel v. Reynolds used the distinction in *Rogers v. Parrey* to separate
reasonable "partial" restraints that applied to a particular town from
unreasonable "general" restraints that applied to the entire kingdom. Such a
distinction made sense in a time when "goodwill" was likely to extend only across
a relatively small region. As discussed below, later cases attempted to apply
this distinction when the relevant trading areas were larger.

Mitchel v. Reynolds approved a parish-wide covenant for a baker. In *Davis
v. Mason*, 5 T.T. 118, 101 Eng. Reg. 69 (K.B. 1793), a covenant extending 10 miles
around Thetford was approved for a surgeon. *Bunn v. Guy*, 4 East 190, 102 Eng.
Rep. 803 (K.B. 1803), upheld a covenant for an attorney extending for a 150 mile
radius around London. *Mallan v. May* upheld a covenant restraining a dentist from
practicing in London. *Harms v. Parsons*, 32 Bev. 328, 55 Eng. Rep. 129 (R.C.
1862), prohibited a horse-hair manufacturer from trading within 200 miles of
Birmingham. *Rousillon v. Rousillon*, 14 Ch. D. 351 (1880), upheld an unlimited
covenant preventing participation in the champagne trade. The clearest
articulation of the test for such cases comes from Chief Justice Tindahl's
decision in *Horner v. Graves*, 7. Bing. 735 (1831):

> We do not see how a better test can be applied to this
> question whether this is or not a reasonable restraint of trade than
> by considering whether the restraint is such only as to afford a
> fair protection to the interests of the party in favor of whom it is
> given, and not so large as to interfere with the interests of the
> public. Whatever restraint is larger than the necessary protection

15

of the party can be of no benefit to either. It can only be oppressive. It is, in the eye of the law, unreasonable. Whatever is injurious to the interests of the public is void on the ground of public policy.

In the United States, *Pierce v. Woodward*, 23 Mass. (6 Pick.) 206 (1828), upheld a covenant for a grocery store operator extending to the city of Boston. *Chappel v. Brockaway*, 211 Wend. 157 (Sup. Ct. N.Y. 1839), upheld a steamship covenant relating to the 100 mile stretch of the Erie Canal from Rochester to Buffalo.[14] In *Oregon Steam Nav. Co. v. Windsor*, 87 U.S. 22 (1874), the U.S. Supreme Court upheld a steamship covenant extending across the state of California. *Watertown Thermometer Co. v. Pool*, 51 Hun. 157, 4 N.Y.S. 861 (1889), upheld an unlimited covenant regarding thermometers.[15] Innovations in the rule of reason continued past the Sherman Act to Chief Justice White's adoption of a market power test for mergers in *Standard Oil*.

While the common law may evolve towards economic efficiency, this does not imply that every innovation in the common law will individually enhance economic efficiency. But it does imply that mistakes in common law decision making (like the decision outlawing vertical restraints in *U. S. v. Arnold, Schwinn & Co.*, 388 U.S. 365 (1967)) are eventually likely to be corrected by further innovations

---

[14] *Kellogg v. Larkin*, 3 Pin. 123 (Wisconsin, 1851), presented another innovation in evaluating restraint of trade cases. This case upheld a city-wide restraint that prohibited a party from engaging in the grain dealing trade. The court indicated that it upheld this restraint only because competition in that trade was available from other parties, thus implicitly applying a market power screen for covenants not to compete similar to that in *Standard Oil*.

[15] See Kintner (1980, at 371-377). Kintner also cites a handful of cases where such constraints were held unreasonable. The distinction between partial and general restraints continued in some form in English law until *Nordenfelt v. Maxim-Nordenfelt Guns and Ammunition Company*, L.R. 1 Ch. 630 (C.A.) (1893) aff'd A.C. 535 (1894), which upheld a world-wide covenant in the sale of armaments. According to Kintner (at 72, fn. 168) in the United States this struggle continued until *Langit v. Sefton Mfg. Co.*, 184 Ill. 326 (1900).

(such as *Continental T.V. Inc. v. GTE Sylvania Inc.*, 433 U.S. 36 (1977), which overturned the *Schwinn* decision.).

The common law on naked restraints seems to have taken such a path. Prior to 1800, price-fixing agreements appear to have been unenforceable no matter what their circumstances. (See, for example, *King v. Norris*, 2 Keny. 300 (1758), and *King v. Eccles*, 1 Leach 274 (1783).) Two cases in the early part of the nineteenth century, *Hearn v. Griffin*, 2 Chitty. 407 (1815), and *Wickens v. Evans*, 17 Q.B. 652 (1827), however, applied the "rule of reason" of *Mitchel v. Reynolds*, and found the relevant contracts valid. Both decisions noted the importance of competitors outside the relevant contractual arrangements.

This line of analysis was rejected, however, in the next important English case, *Hilton v. Eckersley*, 6 E.& B. 47 (1855), where the court opposed all such "naked" restraints as "unreasonable" because they served no positive public purpose. In doing so, the court accepted the position of the defense that "[t]he doctrine laid down in *Mitchel v. Reynolds*, and other cases, that a restraint of trade may be upheld when there is a good consideration for it, is entirely inapplicable to a case where the restraint is itself the consideration."[16] Yet the court in this case implicitly tempered its *per se* rule by explaining (at 76) the economic circumstances of the restraint in question. Not until *Mogul Steamship Co. v. McGregor*, 23 Q.B.D. 598 (1889), *aff'd* A.C. 25 (1892), was the unenforceability of naked restraints made clear in the English common law.

The American common law followed a similar path. In some cases, naked

---

[16] Summary of argument of Mellish for the defense, *Hilton v. Eckersley*, 6 E.& B. 72.

restraints were upheld,[17] while in other cases they were struck down. The most important common law decisions in this field appear to have been the Ohio Supreme Court decision in *Salt Co. v. Guthrie*, 35 Ohio St. 366 (1880) and the New York decision in *People v. Sheldon*, 139 N.Y. 251, 34 N.E. 785 (1893). According to Judge McIlvaine in *Guthrie*

> The clear tendency of such an agreement is to establish a monopoly, and to destroy competition in trade, and for that reason, on the ground of public policy, courts will not aid in its enforcement. It is no answer to say that competition in the salt trade was not in fact destroyed, or that the price of the commodity was not unreasonably advanced. Courts will not stop to inquire as to the degree of injury inflicted upon the public. It is enough to know that the inevitable tendency of such contracts is injurious to the public.

Similarly, Chief Justice Andrews in *Sheldon* stated:

> If agreements and combinations to prevent competition in prices are or may be harmful to trade, the only sure remedy is to prohibit all agreements of that character. If the validity of such an agreement was made to depend on actual proof of public prejudice or injury, it would be very difficult in any case to establish the invalidity, although the moral evidence might be very convincing.

The analyses in *Guthrie* and *Sheldon* would serve as important underpinnings for Taft's Appeals Court decision in *Addyston Pipe*.

Thus, the common law innovation of "reasonableness" for price-fixing contracts and other naked restraints failed. It failed because, unlike the

---

[17] See, for example, *Commonwealth v. Carlisle* Bright., N.P. 36 (Pa. 1821), *Lee v. Louisville Pilot Benevolent & Relief Ass'n*, 65 Ky. 254 (1867), and *Skrainka v. Scharringhausen*, 8 Mo. 522 (1880). Kintner (1980 at 93) refers to the courts that upheld naked restraints as "a small minority of jurisdictions." Recently Grady (1992) has made several efficiency arguments for these decisions. In particular, Grady suggests that the courts were either using a market power screen or allowing agreements that solved "core" problems that may exist in some competitive markets.

rationale presented in *Mallan v. May*, no compelling public policy argument could be made for upholding such covenants to counterbalance their clear anticompetitive potential. Given this, and the administrative difficulties in enforcing any "reasonableness" criteria, Taft's *Addyston Pipe* decision stands to this day.

3. "Law and Economics" and Lande's Analysis

In light of this background of common law and Law and Economics, it is important to review Lande's analysis. Lande contends that Congress was not familiar with the term "economic efficiency." This may be true, but it does not appear of great relevance. The common law, and its opposition to monopoly, dates back several centuries.[18] If there is any validity to the "Law and Economics" school, scholars and judges like Bentham and Holmes were striving for hundreds of years to generate economic efficiency without employing that particular terminology. In effect, they knew intuitively what efficiency was, and were unwilling to wait for economists to define it. As Landes and Posner (1987 at 23) put it, "[p]eople can apply the principles of economics intuitively - and thus "do" economics without knowledge they are doing it." Indeed, the common law cases cited above often refer to such ideas as "the public good," or "the ground of public policy," concepts that may well be good proxies for modern idea of economic efficiency. The fact that Congress did not use the term "economic efficiency" in the debate on the Sherman Act does not imply that economic efficiency was not the underlying goal of the Sherman Act.

Lande's emphasis on this point seems somewhat misplaced. He claims that

---

[18] Cooter and Ulen (1988 at 72) cite the Norman invasion of 1066 as the traditional starting date for the common law.

while legislators knew about the "rectangle" generated by monopoly, they were unaware of the existence of the "triangle" of allocative inefficiency. This is equivalent to saying that Congress was unaware that, as price rises, quantity produced falls and wealth declines. This concept would appear sufficiently straightforward for a late nineteenth century Congressman to understand. Indeed, as Bork (1966 at 16) points out, Senator Sherman was certainly aware of this phenomenon.[19]

Lande's second point is that Congress generally passes laws that do not enhance economic efficiency. In a narrow sense this may be true, but even in the modern era Congress passes laws for economic efficiency, and Rubin gives us reason to believe that this was more likely to occur in 1890.[20,21]

This still leaves unanswered the question of how a nineteenth century Congress would have debated a measure designed to promote economic efficiency. That is, how would they have articulated such a goal in the lexicon of contemporaneous political rhetoric? From a common law framework, they would have noted that the economy had evolved so that consumers could no longer adequately protect their property rights. They would then discuss how the new measure would restore these rights. This is precisely what the main focus of the debates (as presented by both Bork and Lande) was, although naturally the actual rhetoric was

---

[19] According to Sherman, his bill would "protect commerce, nullify contracts that restrain commerce, turn it from its natural course, increase the price of articles, and thereby diminish the amount of commerce." 21 Congressional Record 2462 (1890).

[20] Rubin's analysis also refutes the previous conjecture in Section II-C on why Congress might not be interested in the long-run redistribution of monopoly profits to consumers. A Congress interested in efficiency would not suffer from myopia.

[21] Indeed, Wittman (1989) argues that in general policies in democratic countries tend to reach towards economic efficiency.

somewhat more heated. Thus, an examination of the congressional debates cannot be expected to discern between the efficiency and the welfare-of-consumer hypotheses.

Of course, if Congress were intent on redistributing rents to consumers that would have accrued to producers under the common law, the debate would have also been on these lines. But consider the modern debates over trucking and airline deregulation.[22] They focused on aiding consumers. Yet those laws were clearly designed to enhance economic efficiency. Had Congress wanted to redistribute rents to consumers, they could have arranged to subsidize air travel and truck shipments. Instead, Congress merely restored to consumers the property rights that would generate effective competition.

Consider this issue in light of the recent economic literature on crime enforcement. A policeman might view preventing crime as his job. An economist (as in Becker, 1968) would view the policeman's job as one of efficiently preventing crime. Such a distinction may have little meaning to a policeman with limited resources in a high crime area. Under either view of his role, he is unlikely to spend a good deal of effort fighting jaywalking.

Suppose that because of some exogenous shock (for example, a change in tastes), consumption of illegal narcotics declines. The policeman, now with a surplus of resources, might pursue an (over)vigorous enforcement policy for jaywalkers to justify his budget. In support of his policy he might point towards the legislative debate on the relevant statute, which showed a great concern for the rights of motorists and little or no concern for the rights of jaywalkers who might get in their way. Yet this does not provide convincing evidence that the legislature meant to proscribe all jaywalking to protect the

---

[22] See, for example, Robyn (1987 at 26-56) and Behrman (1980 at 96-103).

rights of motorists. Similarly, an expressed concern for consumers in the debates over the Sherman Act does not imply that Congress was uninterested in the rights of producers.[23]

Almost all legal theories of antitrust are driven by economic theories. The collapse in the mid- and late 1970s of the economic consensus for many antitrust policies was the natural precursor to the reduced antitrust enforcement levels of the 1980s. Despite this dramatic change in the relevant academic thinking, the 1970s antitrust "infrastructure", both public and private, remains largely in place. This infrastructure, looking to increase its own value and represented by Lande, would naturally look to the Congressional debates and note the concern for consumers, just as the policeman discussed above would note the concern of his legislature for motorists. Their success would lead to a greater role for antitrust, at least in the short term. The distinction between protecting consumers and protecting consumers efficiently, which may not have been important given the antitrust consensus of the 1960s and early 1970s, therefore takes on a greater relevance today than it did when Bork wrote his article in the mid-1960s.

To summarize, the Sherman Act can be viewed as a logical extension of the common law. The common law can be seen as an instrument for promoting economic efficiency. Therefore, Congress likely intended for the antitrust laws to enhance efficiency rather than facilitate wealth transfers. The debate on the Sherman Act can be viewed as part of attempts by lawmakers to recapture for consumers the rights to which they were entitled under common law in order to generate efficient outcomes.

---

[23] Rule and Meyer (1988 at 689) make a similar argument.

IV. Support for and Implementation of the Sherman Act

A. Political Support for the Sherman Act

According to the theory of wealth-distributing legislation (for example, Olson, 1965, 1982), some type of strong interest group lobbying effort is necessary to enact legislation that redistributes rents. Conceptually, an interest group such as the "consumer activists" or "consumerists" loosely associated with Ralph Nader, which arose in the late 1960s and early 1970s, could have promoted a consumer rent-seeking antitrust measure. No such group, however, appears to have been a crucial supporter of the Sherman Act. The closest and most important consumer-type group that scholars (DiLorenzo, 1985, Stigler, 1985, and Thorelli, 1955 at 58-60) record from the 1880s and 1890s are the Grangers, a populist movement that was devoted largely to lowering railroad rates for farmers.

As Stigler (1985) points out, however, it is difficult to conclude that the Grangers were the primary motivation behind the Sherman Act. The Grangers had already obtained their desired legislation in 1887, the Interstate Commerce Act, which established the Interstate Commerce Commission (ICC) to reallocate rents to farmers.[24] It is reasonable to believe that the Grangers approved of the Sherman Act, since it was not inconsistent with their interests. Yet the Grangers did not have a larger stake in its passage than any other group and it was not certain at the time of its passage whether the Sherman Act would apply

---

[24] See Hovenkamp (1988) and Gilligan, Marshall, and Weingast (1989). As several scholars have noted, the Grangers were aided by the railroads themselves, who also served to benefit from the legislation. For a full description of the political and economic forces behind the Interstate Commerce Act, see Fiorina (1986), Gilligan, Marshall, and Weingast (1989) and Prager (1989).

to railroads.[25] As discussed above in Section II, Lande appears also to believe that populist sentiment was not responsible for the Sherman Act, as he is clear in his view that the Act was not a measure for distributing wealth from richer to poorer segments of society.[26]

The support for the Sherman Act came from a great many sources and was widespread. Indeed, the vote for the final bill in Congress was nearly unanimous.[27] A number of states across the country passed their own antitrust measures during the same time period in a pattern unrelated to Granger activity across states (Stigler 1985 at 5-6). This is consistent with a broad-based desire for economic efficiency achieved by making a moderate change in public policy through amending the common law (as discussed by Stigler, 1985 at 7) or by an efficiency generating compromise among interest groups, as described by Becker (1983) and Wittman (1989). The Act does not seem to have been generated by the activity typically associated with rent-seeking legislation.

B. Implementation

Modern political economy also posits that the goals of a particular policy will affect how Congress chooses to implement that policy. Congress' designation

---

[25] This question was not resolved until *U.S. v. Trans-Missouri Freight Association* 166 U.S. 290 (1897).

[26] If indeed wealth redistribution were the goal of the Sherman Act, it would raise some difficult policy questions. For instance, assume that two ski resorts, each owned by a labor union pension fund, desired to merge for market power reasons. Assuming that the clientele of these resorts have higher average income than the union members, a wealth transfer policy might imply that such a case should not be brought.

[27] In the House, the vote was 242 for, none against. In the Senate the vote was 52 for and 1 against (Stigler 1985 at 5). As Stigler notes, however, there were a large number of Congressmen who abstained, which may have been an implicit form of opposition.

of the judicial system to interpret the antitrust laws suggests a stronger likelihood that Congress desired economic efficiency to be the goal of the Sherman Act.

Two basic methods were available to Congress in implementing the Sherman Act.[28] First, it could have entrusted the law to the judiciary, as with the common law. Under this arrangement, decisions would be made by judges under the "preponderance of the evidence" or "greater weight of the evidence" standard generally used in civil cases. (See, for example, Cleary, 1972 at 793-796.) Granting courts the authority to determine the meaning of a vaguely worded law such as the Sherman Act is entirely consistent with the precepts of a common law approach promoting economic efficiency.[29]

Alternatively, Congress could have entrusted the enforcement of the statute to an administrative agency such as the ICC. An administrative agency, as defined here, would create and enforce its own law by making decisions and creating rules. (See, in general, Stewart, 1975). Its actions would be subject to review by the judiciary, but only on a "reasoned consistency" or "arbitrary and capricious" standard.[30] Under such a standard, a court would generally uphold an agency's decision if due process procedures were followed, if there

---

[28] The analysis in this section, of course, simplifies somewhat the nature of the implementation question open to Congress.

[29] The criterion employed by judges may be economic efficiency, as discussed above in Section III. While there is dispute in the literature, it would seem that judges have at least some incentives to seek efficient outcomes that maximize wealth. See the discussion in Cooter and Rubinfeld (1989 at 1091-2). This hypothesis has been empirically supported in Anderson, Shughart, and Tollison (1989). Congress could also give specific instructions for rent-distribution in a statute and then have the judiciary enforce the statute. The antitrust laws, however, contain no such instruction.

[30] See, for example, *Greater Boston Television Corporation v. F.C.C.* 444 F.2d. 850-853 (1970), *Chevron U.S.A. Inc. v. National Resource Defense Council, Inc.* 467 U.S. 837 (1984) and Stewart (1975 at 1680), as well as 5 U.S.C. Section 706(2)(A).

were a reasonable basis to support the agency's decision, and if the agency is acting in a consistent manner.[31]

The early academic theory of administrative agencies argued that such agencies would be more efficient administrators of one part of the law than judges, who have to deal with a wide variety of matters. (For a summary of this rationale see Mitnick, 1980 at 31.) This idea has been replaced by the "capture" theory.[32] According to the capture theory, Congress establishes an administrative agency to enforce the political "deal" it has enacted. The agency then adopts a set of administrative procedures to enforce the political contract.

Under this arrangement, should an agency's future political leadership attempt to undo the original congressional political arrangement, it would have to overcome the institutional arrangements already in place. Existing administrative procedures would require a large amount of both time and agency resources to surmount, so that the future leadership of the agency would find it difficult to depart from the mission Congress intended. Similarly, the political deal would be protected from the courts by the "reasoned consistency" standard and from a new legislative political equilibrium by complicated legislative procedures. (See Shepsle, 1979, McCubbins, Noll, and Weingast, 1987, and Bishop,

---

[31] A good example of this difference can be seen in Judge Richard Posner's decision for the Court of Appeals in *United Air Lines v. CAB* 766 F.2d 1107 (1985). (This case concerned the Civil Aeronautics Board's restrictions on the use of display preference in airline computer reservation systems on competitive grounds.) In upholding the CAB, the Court indicated that while it had substantial doubts about the CAB's conclusions on the competitive implications of display preference, all the law required was that the CAB make a finding based on an "arbitrary and capricious" standard, not on the preponderance of the evidence.

[32] See Stigler (1970), Posner (1972), Fiorina (1986), and McCubbins, Noll, and Weingast (1987). For a discussion along similar lines from a different point of view see Epstein (1985 at 263-282). Benson and Greenhut (1986) also use a "political economy" approach to analyze antitrust enforcement, though they reach somewhat different conclusions.

1990.) In effect, the administrative procedures create a bias towards the client interest group in the administrative agency's decisions.

The rise of administrative agencies in the twentieth century is consistent with Rubin's thesis on the goals of law in an era of interest groups. The "capture theory" explains why Behrman (1980 at 115-6) found that administrative procedures constituted a significant obstacle to the Civil Aeronautics Board's (CAB) internal deregulation effort in the late 1970s. It is also consistent with the abolition of the CAB as a result of the Airline Deregulation Act of 1978 and the elimination of almost all of the ICC's trucking responsibilities in the Motor Carrier Act of 1980 (Behrman, 1980 at 75, and Robyn, 1987).

Congress already had administrative agencies in its legislative arsenal in 1890, having created the first federal one (the ICC) three years earlier in 1887.[33] Further, the British and the European Community[34] experience indicates that there is no inherent reason why antitrust matters cannot be given to an administrative agency. Thus, if Congress sought to redistribute rents to consumers, theory indicates that it would have set up an administrative agency to enforce its goal.[35] Instead, Congress created the right of private and public action to allow judicial enforcement of the Sherman Act.

---

[33] Fiorina (1986 at 36, fn. 5) points out that by 1887 several states had extensive experience with regulatory commissions.

[34] Scherer (1980 at 505) and Kerse (1981 at 27).

[35] In the 1887 debates over the Interstate Commerce Act, the pro-consumer House of Representatives preferred a measure that would outlaw pooling in order to reduce railroad prices. The House also wanted the measure to be enforced by the judiciary because an administrative agency would be likely to be captured by railroad interests. The pro-railroad Senate, on the other hand, desired an administrative agency with no anti-pooling mandate. The final compromise created the ICC and banned pooling (see Fiorina, 1986 at 38 and Gilligan, Marshall and Weingast, 1989 at 48). The ban on pooling was effectively extended to the rest of the economy through the Sherman Act and the decision in *Addyston Pipe* 12 years later.

Conceivably administrative agencies could have been considered an oddity in 1890 (though they were common at the state level) and Congress may have been reluctant to create another one without first evaluating the ICC's performance. Twenty-four years later, however, in 1914, the Congress created the Federal Trade Commission to also enforce the antitrust laws, as well as to handle consumer protection matters. At first glance, the FTC, with its Commissioners and administrative law judges, looks like an administrative agency. Yet when it comes to antitrust matters, FTC cases use the same body of law as Justice Department cases and are also reviewed by appeals courts on a "preponderance of the evidence" standard.[36] By itself, the FTC, like the Department of Justice, does not have the legal authority to stop a merger, declare an industry trade practice anticompetitive, or create law contrary to established precedent without substantial reason. As Posner (1970 at 71) once described the agencies' role in the judicial process, "[i]n both cases, the agencies merely propose and the courts dispose."

This is in contrast to the FTC's consumer protection authority under the Magnuson-Moss Act of 1975. Under this law, which is generally credited with "revitalizing" the agency, the FTC can pass consumer protection rules subject to judicial review only under a "reasoned consistency" standard.[37] With this new authority, the FTC spent several years (from 1975 to 1980) passing broad rules

---

[36] Compare, for instance, the decision in *FTC v. Indiana Federation of Dentists*, 745 F.2nd 1124 (1984), where the FTC was overruled by an Appeals Court, to the discretion shown to the Environmental Protection Agency in *Chevron, supra* note 30, which was decided four months earlier.

[37] See, for example, *American Financial Services Association v. F.T.C.*, 767 F. 2d. 957 (1985).

that applied to goods as diverse as funerals and sweaters.[38,39]

The theory presented here indicates that the Magnuson-Moss Act, by giving the FTC clear administrative authority, was supported by narrowly focused political lobbies. In fact, as Hasin (1987) and Muris (1989) point out, the base of support for the Magnuson-Moss Act was the "consumerist" public interest groups associated with Ralph Nader. By 1975 these groups had succeeded in capturing the FTC and they did not trust the judiciary to enforce the political deal they were able to obtain from Congress. Later, as a more efficiency-oriented 1980s FTC tried to undo the work of the 1970s by eliminating several consumer protection rules, its efforts were impaired by the administrative procedures required under the Magnuson-Moss Act.[40]

To summarize, Congress had a choice in 1890 of whether to implement its antitrust policy through either the judiciary or an administrative agency. The entrustment of antitrust decisions to the judiciary in 1890, and again in 1914, suggests that Congress intended economic efficiency to be the goal of the Sherman Act. Had wealth transfers been the goal of the Act, the modern theory of

---

[38] As Hasin (1987 at 11) notes, it is not clear whether the original 1914 Act gave the FTC the authority to write industry regulations for consumer protection purposes. Consequently, the Commission very rarely asserted such powers prior to Magnuson-Moss.

[39] Averitt (1979) has argued that the FTC can bring non-Sherman Act violations under the "unfairness" part of Section 5 of the FTC Act. (Such action would be subject to judicial deference under *American Financial Services, supra* note 37.) In the 1980's, however, the Appeals Courts rejected the idea that Section 5 of the FTC Act reached beyond the scope of the Sherman Act. See *Rueben H. Donnelley Corp. v. F.T.C.* 630 F.2d. 920 (1980), *Boise Cascade Corp. v. F.T.C* 637 F.2d. 573 (1980), *E.I. Du Pont de Nemours v. F.T.C.* 729 F.2d. 128 (1984) and Hobbs (1986).

[40] See, for example, Dissents of Commissioners Mary I. Azcuenaga and Andrew J. Strenio Jr. concerning the "Transistor Rule", 54 <u>Federal Register</u> 1192-3 (June 9, 1989). Commissioners Azcuenaga and Strenio argued that the matter at hand was not important enough to merit devoting the large amount of FTC resources and time that would be required under the Magnuson-Moss Act in order to retract the rule.

administrative agencies suggests that the Congress would have acted as it did when it regulated the railroads in 1887 and embodied antitrust authority in an administrative agency.

V. Conclusion

Theory and empirical evidence strongly indicate that the primary goal of the Sherman Act of 1890 was to enhance economic efficiency. This type of statute was not uncommon before the modern rise of interest groups, nor unknown afterward. The Sherman Act is a logical and modest extension of the common law, which reaches towards economic efficiency. Unlike the Magnuson-Moss Act of 1975, no "consumerist" lobby appears to have exerted enough influence over Congress in 1890 to pass a law that would redistribute wealth via antitrust proceedings. Further, enforcement authority for the Sherman Act was given to the judiciary, rather than to an administrative agency subject to capture by special interests. Thus, the weight of the evidence suggests that the original goal of the Sherman Act was to maximize economic efficiency.

References

Anderson, Gary M., William F. Shughart II, and Robert D. Tollison, "On the Incentives of Judges to Legislate Wealth Transfers," Journal of Law and Economics 32:1 (1989) 215-228.

Averitt, Neil, "The Meaning of 'Unfair Methods of Competition' in Section 5 of Federal Trade Commission," Boston College Law Review 21:227-290 (1979).

Baxter, William F., "Separation of Powers, Prosecutorial Discretion, and the 'Common Law' Nature of Antitrust Law," Texas Law Review 60 (1982) 661-703.

Becker, Gary S., "Crime and Punishment: An Economic Approach," Journal of Political Economy 76:2 (March 1968) 169-217.

Becker, Gary S., "A Theory of Competition Among Pressure Groups for Political Influence," <u>Quarterly Journal of Economics</u> 98 (August 1983) 371-400.

Behrman, Bradley, "Civil Aeronautics Board," in James Q. Wilson (ed.) <u>The Politics of Regulation</u> Basic Books (1980) New York.

Benson, Bruce L., and M.L. Greenhut, "Special Interests, Bureaucrats, and Antitrust: An Explanation of the Antitrust Paradox," in Ronald E. Grieson, ed., <u>Antitrust and Regulation</u> Lexington Books (1986) Lexington, MA.

Bishop, William, "A Theory of Administrative Law," <u>Journal of Legal Studies</u> 19:2, pt. 1 (1990) 489-530.

Bork, Robert H., "Legislative Intent and the Policy of the Sherman Act," <u>Journal of Law and Economics</u> 9:1 (1966) 7-48.

Calvani, Terry, "Consumer Welfare is the Prime Objective of Antitrust," <u>Legal Times</u>, 7 (1984) 14.

Cleary, Edward W. (editor), <u>McCormick's Handbook of the Law of Evidence</u>, West Publishing Co., (1972, second edition) St. Paul, MN.

Commons, John R., "Law and Economics," <u>Yale Law Journal</u> 35 (1925) 371-382.

Constantine, Lloyd, "Antitrust Federalism," <u>Washburn Law Journal</u> 29:2 (1990) 163-184.

Cooter, Robert D., and David L. Rubinfeld, "Economic Analysis of Legal Disputes and Their Resolution," <u>Journal of Economic Literature</u> 27:3 (1989) 1067-1097.

Cooter, Robert D., and Thomas Ulen, <u>Law and Economics</u>, Scott, Foresman, and Company (1988) Glenview, Illinois.

DiLorenzo, Thomas J., "The Origins of Antitrust: An Interest-Group Perspective," <u>International Review of Law and Economics</u> 5 (1985) 73-90.

Easterbrook, Frank, "Workable Antitrust Policy," <u>Michigan Law Review</u> 84 (1986) 1696-1713.

Eaton, "On Contracts in Restraint of Trade," <u>Harvard Law Review</u> 4 (1890) 128-135.

Epstein, Richard A., <u>Takings: Private Property and the Power of Eminent Domain</u>, Harvard (1985) Cambridge MA.

Fiorina, Morris P., "Legislator Uncertainty, Legislative Control, and the Delegation of Legislative Power," <u>Journal of Law, Economics, and Organization</u> 2:1 (1986) 33-51.

Fisher, Alan A., and Robert H. Lande, "Efficiency Considerations in Merger Enforcement," <u>California Law Review</u> 71 (1983) 1580-1696.

Fisher Alan A., Frederick I. Johnson, and Robert H. Lande, "Price Effects of

Horizontal Mergers," California Law Review 77:4 (1989) 777-827.

Friedman, David, "Efficient Institutions for the Private Enforcement of Law," Journal of Legal Studies 13:2 (1984) 379-396.

Grady, Mark F., "Toward A Positive Economic Theory of Antitrust", Economic Inquiry, 30:3 (1992) 225-41.

Gilligan, Thomas W., William J. Marshall, and Barry R. Weingast, "Regulation and the Theory of Legislative Choice: The Interstate Commerce Act of 1887," Journal of Law and Economics 32:1 (1989) 35-61.

Hasin, Bernice Rothman, Consumers, Commissions, and Congress: Law, Theory and the Federal Trade Commission, 1968-1985, Transaction Books (1987) New Brunswick, New Jersey.

Hobbs, Caswell O., "Antitrust in the Next Decade - A Role For the Federal Trade Commission," 31 Antitrust Bulletin 31:451-480 (1986).

Holmes, Oliver Wendall, Jr., The Common Law (Mark DeWolfe Howe, ed.) Harvard University Press (1963) Cambridge, MA. First published by Little, Brown and Co. (1881) Boston MA.

Hovenkamp, Herbert, "Regulatory Conflict in the Gilded Age: Federalism and the Railroad Problem," Yale Law Journal 97 (1988) 1017-1072.

Kerse, C.S., EEC Antitrust Procedure, European Law Centre, LTD. (1981) London.

Kintner, Earl W., Federal Antitrust Law (Volume 1) Anderson Publishing, Cincinnati (1980).

Kovacic, William E., "The Antitrust Paradox Revisited: Robert Bork and the Transformation of Modern Antitrust Policy," Wayne Law Review 36:4 (1990) 1413-1471.

Lande, Robert H., "Wealth Transfers as the Original and Primary Concern of Antitrust: The Efficiency Interpretation Challenged," Hastings Law Journal 34 (1982) 65-131.

Landes, William M., and Richard A. Posner, The Economic Structure of Tort Law, Harvard University Press (1987) Cambridge MA.

Letwin, William L, "The English Common Law Regarding Monopolies," University of Chicago Law Review 21:3 (1954) 355-385.

May, James, "Antitrust Practices and Procedure in the Formative Era: The Constitutional and Conceptual Reach of State Antitrust Law 1880-1918," University of Pennsylvania Law Review 135:3 (1987) 495-593.

McCubbins, Matthew D., Roger G. Noll, and Barry R. Weingast, "Administrative Procedures as Instruments of Political Control," Journal of Law, Economics, and Organization 3:2 (Fall 1987) 243-277.

Mitnick, B.M., *The Political Economy of Regulation: Creating, Designing, and Removing Regulatory Forms*, New York (1980) Columbia University Press.

Muris, Timothy J., "The Federal Trade Commission at 75," mimeo, George Mason University (1989).

Oliver, Daniel, "Statement of Chairman Oliver," *Antitrust Law Review* 57:1 (1988) 235-244.

Olson, Mancur, *The Logic of Collective Action*, Cambridge MA (1965) Harvard Press.

Olson, Mancur, *The Rise and Decline of Nations: Economic Growth, Stagflation, and Social Rigidities*, New Haven, CT (1982) Yale University Press.

Oppenheim, S. Chesterfield, Glen E. Weston, and J. Thomas McCarthy, *Federal Antitrust Laws: Cases, Text, and Commentary*, St. Paul, MN (1981, fourth edition) West Publishing Co.

Prager, Robin A., "Using Stock Price Data to Measure the Effects of Regulation: The Interstate Commerce Act and the Railroad Industry," *Rand Journal of Economics* 20:2 (1989) 280-290.

Posner, Richard A., "Do We Really Need an FTC," *Antitrust Law and Economics Review* 3:3 (1970) 65-98.

Posner, Richard A., "The Behavior of Administrative Agencies," *Journal of Legal Studies* 1:2 (1972) 305-347.

Posner, Richard A., "The Social Costs of Monopoly and Regulation," *Journal of Political Economy* 83:4 (September 1975) 807-827.

Posner, Richard A., *Economic Analysis of Law*, Little, Brown, and Company (1986, 3rd ed.) Boston.

Robyn, Dorothy, *Breaking the Special Interests*, University of Chicago Press (1987) Chicago.

Rubin, Paul H., "Common Law and Statute Law," *Journal of Legal Studies* 11:2 (June 1982) 205-223.

Rubin, Paul H., *Business Firms and the Common Law: The Evolution of Efficient Rules* Praeger (1983) New York.

Rule, Charles F. and David L. Meyer, "An Antitrust Enforcement Policy to Maximize the Wealth of All Consumers," *Antitrust Bulletin* 33 (Winter 1988) 677-712.

Scherer, F.M., *Industrial Market Structure and Economic Performance*, Rand McNally (1980) Chicago.

Shepsle, Kenneth A., "Institutional Arrangements and Equilibrium in Multidimensional Voting Models," *American Journal of Political Science* 23:1 (February 1979) 27-59.

Shoven, John B. and John Whalley, "Applied General-Equilibrium Models of Taxation and International Trade: An Introduction and Survey," Journal of Economic Literature 22:3 (September 1984) 1007-1051.

Stewart, Richard B., "The Reformation of Administrative Law," Harvard Law Review 88 (1975) 1669-1813.

Stigler, George, "The Theory of Economic Regulation," Bell Journal of Economics 2:1 (1970) 3-21.

Stigler, George, "The Origins of the Sherman Act," Journal of Legal Studies 14:1 (January 1985) 1-12.

Thorelli, Hans, The Federal Antitrust Policy: Origination of an American Tradition (1955).

Tollison, Robert, and Robert McCormick, Politicians, Legislation, and the Economy, Boston (1981) Martinus Niuhoff.

Toulmine, Harry A., A Treatise on the Antitrust Laws of the United States Cincinnati (1949) W.H. Anderson and Company.

Williamson, Oliver, "Economies as a Welfare Defense: The Welfare Tradeoffs," American Economic Review 58:1 (March 1968) 18-36.

Williamson, Oliver, "Economies as An Antitrust Defense Revisited," University of Pennsylvania Law Review 125 (1977) 699-736.

Wittman, Donald, "Why Democracies Produce Efficient Results," Journal of Political Economy 97:6 (December 1989) 1395-1424.